PRAISE FOR *CITY OF EVES*

"*City of Eves* is a stunning, lyrical meditation of self, history, human relation, and world. Photo albums give way to questions of God. Love pervades every turn. We see the complexity of self and identity, the intergenerational gaze, landscapes, both past and present. 'I wanted the world to speak,' Bonilla writes, 'but it was just me and my thoughts, and iron pressing the chest.'"

—**Bianca Stone**, author of *What Is Otherwise Infinite*

"Silvia Bonilla's language is furiously alive, rippling with startling imagery. The linguistic intensity enacts the slippages and beauty of belonging—Sonia and her friends live in a whirlwind of poverty, in the din of gender norms. Bonilla reveals the necessity of migration but also sets nostalgia in motion. Interiority is vividly felt: it's luminous, barbed. Bonilla's debut is brilliant, singular."

—**Eduardo C. Corral**, author of *Guillotine*

"*City of Eves* is a keen exploration of womanhood, culture, and identity. The collection sings deep truths and elicits 'walking dreams' with which to consider the Eves we've known and carried."

—**Gloria Muñoz**, author of *Danzirly*

"Silvia Bonilla's *City of Eves* makes visceral the precarity and hardship that accompanies immigration from South America to the United States where poverty and its hungers, accompanied by the intersections of race and gender, remains a violence."

—**Brenda Cárdenas**, author of *Trace*

"Silvia Bonilla's *City of Eves* is a book of haunting precision and simmering brilliance. Spare and atmospheric, these poems investigate lovers, curses, hunger, possibility, poverty, migration, identity, transformation, and stasis. We meet parents, then meet children, then contemplate God. Narratives run together incisively; they split and then reconvene. One poem references the 'shivering act / of happiness'; another announces, 'I came loose from my past.' Bonilla's keen powers of observation, sense, and sound are just what we need right now."

—**Natalie Shapero**, author of *Popular Longing*

CITY OF EVES

Camino del Sol

A Latinx Literary Series

Rigoberto González, Series Editor

SILVIA BONILLA

City of Eves

Poems

TUCSON

The University of Arizona Press
www.uapress.arizona.edu

We respectfully acknowledge the University of Arizona is on the land and territories of Indigenous peoples. Today, Arizona is home to twenty-two federally recognized tribes, with Tucson being home to the O'odham and the Yaqui. The University strives to build sustainable relationships with sovereign Native Nations and Indigenous communities through education offerings, partnerships, and community service.

ISBN-13: 978-0-8165-5577-2 (paperback)
ISBN-13: 978-0-8165-5578-9 (ebook)

Cover design by Leigh McDonald
Cover image by Sara Jaramillo
Designed and typeset by Leigh McDonald in Goudy Old Style 10.5/14 and Ainslie Sans (display)

Publication of this book is made possible in part by the proceeds of a permanent endowment created with the assistance of a Challenge Grant from the National Endowment for the Humanities, a federal agency.

Library of Congress Cataloging-in-Publication Data
Names: Bonilla, Silvia author
http://id.loc.gov/authorities/names/no2022108677
Title: City of eves : poems / Silvia Bonilla.
Description: Tucson : University of Arizona Press, 2026. | Series: Camino del sol: a Latinx literary series
Identifiers: LCCN 2025007464 (print) | LCCN 2025007465 (ebook) | ISBN 9780816555772 paperback | ISBN 9780816555789 ebook
Subjects: LCGFT: Poetry
http://id.loc.gov/authorities/genreForms/gf2014026481
Classification: LCC PS3602.O657325 C58 2026 (print) | LCC PS3602.O657325 (ebook) | DDC 811/.6—dc23/eng/20250425
LC record available at https://lccn.loc.gov/2025007464
LC ebook record available at https://lccn.loc.gov/2025007465

Printed in the United States of America
♾ This paper meets the requirements of ANSI/NISO Z39.48-1992 (Permanence of Paper).

Contents

PART II

PART III

PART IV

Foreword

A young woman named Sonia from Guayaquil, Ecuador, comes of age in these pages, best friends Irene and Matilde by her side: "Like sisters, our shared condition / is poverty, / rustling over our / bodies." As they mature, they realize that these bodies can be sources of power, particularly in the pursuits of love and money. Sonia, for example, makes use of her feminine beauty to model at the Art Institute. It's a rare moment of agency and a departure from the limited paths available to poor women who, like Matilde, marry young or, like the Eves, charge for the pleasure of their company. Sonia wants "more than asphalt underneath [her] feet," but sometimes dreams are hindered by reality. She soon finds herself in a familiar and devastating situation: single motherhood after her sweetheart's life "was stopped by a bullet."

Like her mother before her, Sonia must contend with tough questions—"How do I break from this town? From my daughter?"—to rebuild her life. Such challenging choices are gut-wrenching, and it's a state of despair that will be echoed repeatedly on her journey to the United States and during her early years laboring in a promised land that demands much sacrifice:

I need my heart to shoot out
like an arrow, to leave the body
by the cobwebs or otherwise
send it back in a cardboard coffin.

The most compelling characteristic of Silvia Bonilla's *City of Eves* is its unwillingness to be summarized so easily. Sonia's is a story about growing up, but it is also about the trials of womanhood and about immigration. Reading this book is like flipping through a photo album, an activity we find a young Sonia doing in the opening poems. Like her, we too must fill in the blanks in the stories with our imaginations, because many of the other narrators are silent, missing, or no longer alive to complete the tales. Yet these glimpses into the complex lives of women come steeped in charged emotions, like the feelings of abandonment, bewilderment, and, mercifully, triumph. Though the lines "Women move through time and place, / alone in the dark" weigh heavily on the tone of the book, so does the phrase "We are in a new state of affection." Even the deepest wounds can heal.

Bonilla's debut dares to center the stories of women who thrive outside of conventional gender expectations, but also present are those women who find purpose in them. Our task as readers is, not to judge, but to understand the social and financial circumstances that constrict movement or force people away. To leave or to remain—who's to say what's the better proposition, *City of Eves* posits, when neither offers any guarantees of happiness or success? Sonia wonders about this as she settles into a new normal in the North. Like every memory in that photo album, the thought is bittersweet.

—RIGOBERTO GONZÁLEZ

CITY OF EVES

PART I

La Bahía, Guayaquil

In the morning, Irene, Matilde, and I flock to the sound of opening bells.
There's salt and blood in the breathing holes of fish and a bubble
like a word caught in the last breath before death.

All signs spell *fresh* at the market. We come early on our way to school.
I inhale the rusty smell of pig's blood and watch
the heart under the knife. I shift my eyes to the sunflower stand:
quick, make it quick, promise to never to eat one of your kind.

We walk the dark corners, stand after stand filled with the world's gifts:
lipsticks from Spain, bras from Colombia, and kohl
we'll burn the tips of to make even darker cat eyes.

We hold our purses to armpits;
not Matilde, who keeps a *monedero*
in her bra and a cigarette on her lips.

She pokes the animals as if to wake them up,
covers the tuna's eyes—*they're too revealing of his*
suffering.

She kisses the boar's feet, *your excellence!* and bows,
on freshness, only the skin can testify.

We stroll and dream of the exciting lives
playing out outside this country.

Bleaching cream gets pulled from the shelf, and Matilde
holds it to her face and laughs; her coarse laugh
is wind with danger in it.

Someone sprays perfume, and the mist swirls inside the cone of
light filtering from holes in the roof.

At night, the quietness of a sterile city.

Our wishes rest on beds spritzed with boiled lavender.
The world, the world turns into a departing ship.

If a Birth Certificate Was at Hand

it'd have read something like:

Father: boy who listened to her sadness.
Mother: girl who rattled her woes at him.

When she got a contraction,

lights flickered, and when she called God
a criminal–

they pulled me out.

They wouldn't have a name for me
until they saw the birthmark.
Sonia, she said, screaming.

Anyone can have a baby,
she would've been told by the nurse

extracting mucus
from my nose.

They would've had pity
for both girls,

settling
like stray cats,

inflamed nipples,
mouths eager and angry.

Mora, or Unbaptized

Hoping to be accepted into Catholic school,
Sonia asks for her baptismal certificate.

At the rectory,
Sonia's grandma fills out what she can.

The priest needs more—
but family facts are not available.

Why a mora *at this age?*
Is she a product of the following:

solicitation—
infidelity—

rape—

Aren't we all a product of rape?
Seven words—
the loud flock from her grandma's mouth.

The Holy ponders over,
walks out.

Under his tunic—
cock gets big then flat.

Before You Ask God, Thank Him

Wing-beat variation,
a dove's moans,
all afternoon.

When we sing,
our voices pitch bull-like hardiness.

We hear stories from a book of pain,
as if we didn't know.

In the alleyways of our history books
someone was always running, clicking

their heels along the whitewashed gloom.

We kneel down, take
Communion–

no iron roots
at the ankle–

a Bible opened to Psalm 106.

Language Arts

It was charity from the gringos.
The beach camp where us girls met,
watching seafoam make passes
at our toes for hours.
Even asleep at night, we felt as if the slow waving
of water carried us.
There was language instruction; our tongues
weeping, we repeated and repeated.
The barn roof echoing.
No need to translate us,
our skin testified to its nagging past:
mulata, chola, india.

Sonia's Family Tree

There is one picture of their shotgun wedding at the courthouse.
The lighting is unfavorable. She smiles. His face is rude, red.
My mother is just a mass in my grandmother's belly. The A-line
dress shows a curve. They have two witnesses.
And God, of course, who must have been there. Blessed is she
among many women with absent partners.

There is no date on the picture, nothing from earth in her hands.
She leans forward to sign her name as someone's wife.
The desk has a pile of yellow folders, the country's flag,
and what seems to be
a half-empty cup of coffee.

Touring Banana Fields in a Photograph of My Grandfather

From highway to junction
centuries change.

A dog eats a dog named Lola eats a bone.

Wind rides out, swirls
to cordon Lola with gravel dust.

My grandmother describes it as *stained glass.*

There he is, she says, pointing at him
and the other boys who labored there.

Smoking, backs to the edge
of a landscape

golden

caught quickly
squinting at the sun.

Last Photo of Sonia's Grandmother

in the photo albums that got lost somehow.
Inside her eyelids, she saved our whole lives.
Her face was both tender and embittered, her bones
turned you into a music box as you walked.
She waited for a daughter
who never returned. She called to her,
talking to someone only she saw. In our place,
one melody: her name.
She sat on the wicker chair by the window, insomniac.
Talking to Jesus, exchanging promises for her return.
What kind of deal was that? When she hadn't much to offer.

We Say God

has stolen from us so many times it is now a
habit. After an afternoon of rain, that last rumble
hatches. A partial rainbow, ready,
and we sit at the promenade and wish to open
the thick woven totes that fell from the sky.
Our prizes.
Sometimes a plane is a distraction.
In the distance, a murmur. And all the unblinking eyes,
windows.

Sonia Borrowed

a uniform from Irene for a month.
A white poplin blouse and blue skirt.

She waited in her slip for her friend's steps
on the patio and went out to meet her.

Once they switched, Sonia ran to catch the bus, carrying with her
the half moons of Irene's sweat.

I'm in the afternoon classes, she explains to the driver
who says she can't ride after 12:00 p.m.

Everyone's eyes on her, she sits next to a woman
with a baby spread over her legs.

She shakes, and the baby hums.
Sonia wishes she could bring her mother back.

These are ugly times, her grandmother says, every day,
shaking her head.

Just share for a month, until I get the check.

Sonia believed everything she said when she stood in the kitchen
with the promise of a meal.

Beauty in the Dead

Photos of deceased family hung in Irene's living room.
The dead and their rosaries overhanging their fingers like clipped art.

<u>Grandparents</u> <u>Drowned Boy, Infant</u> <u>Young Man in Military Attire</u>

All who enter the mysterious world of heavens
will be greeted by angels
reads the plaque under the pictures.

I'll want my grandma in a white satin dress,
her gray-streaked hair pulled back.

I'm thinking she'll want more of the terrestrial,
color in her lips and on her nails.

None of her human suffering visible.
Only a divine tale.

They Watch Us from Inside Lighted Museum Boxes

To leave our plotted land and keep
walking toward campgrounds far away,
patches we'd only seen in movies. Who wanted
us erased? All those *immaculate* bones
buried in our church tunnels
are such puzzles for which cement
was the better option. Who looked down,
praising oneself: *everything's going as planned.*
So much grief had to give roots eventually.
Who made holes to bury loved ones, to hide richness.
This is old grief—we watch now from outside
the glass.

Sonia Passes a Note During Math Class

As if I miss
myself, I write to
myself.

As if a stranger ties her life
to mine.

When I wear her uniform,
my quiet shade

becomes her loud shadow.

Like sisters, our shared condition
is poverty,

rustling over our
bodies.

The rope,
the loud punch

that makes us
hang our heads
down.

Matilde says, *we need new talents,*
look like angels or
look for angels.

Stop wasting time kissing farm boys!
Learn to undress shutting your eyes.

Sonia's Diary

Rain falling on

aluminum roof

piercing like nails

heavy like shots

or stomps.

It's hard to sleep.

I met a boy.

Our Neighborhoods and Other Neighborhoods

A few streets divided us, but we found each other
through barking dogs, fern-covered houses.

At the bus stop, class didn't matter.
It was what heaven might be like: *garments mixed,*

a medal for the neck of the looter.
And to every man, a woman or two. We laughed.

Teenage wolves
passed around

a cigarette.

Wet flesh was all the same. No color prevailed—
we learned to kiss, to hold

tongue and joint—white horn,
that crescent moon.

Rich kids had an aggressiveness
about them, having shopped for love with their
fathers.

What was snaked in the old ground—turning,
turning once more.

Clandestine

Tobacco from the bazaar on Lemon Street
We placed all the change we had
between his fingers and watched
the silent grotto of his eyes
for an answer.
Taking the first glacial inhale—
filling our chests

we blew out with tight lips.

Ocean spitting from the esophagus
to rocks of yellow seaweed mane.

We burnt our childhood
to hang on ash.

Posthumous

Sometimes your rage and dark,
volatile mood reached me

with more than a cotton dishcloth.

Your plan to escape poverty: a jar of coins.

And you didn't want to believe how poor we were.
And I wanted more than asphalt underneath my feet.

You were the wax leopard-skin idol
I held onto when you were unsure

of what to call me.

I called you Sonia, our name.

This morning, canaries zigzag a pool left by heavy rain;
I come loose from my past.

There,

at the roundabout.
If you are hungry, come by the house,
Irene whispers
in my ear.

Days we met after school,
laughing at the male drivers
whose eyes
diverted from the wheel
to scan our bodies.
Car after car,
calling us,
what name?

The Femininity of Music

Matilde and I couldn't afford the show.
Irene claimed her dad said, *too expensive!*

We knew she was lying,
that she skipped in solidarity.

We sketched on notebooks the possibilities:
T-shirts with press-on pictures of Maná,
uniform skirts rolled high up our waists.

From the rock radio station: *are they really here?*
This tease gave us goosebumps.

Maná meant supernatural!
Blessings! Power! A virus

of darkness we wished would strike
us, and the yawning of our city.

From then on, we became suspicious
of humility, believing we'd been born

to escape.

We stood outside the stadium,
all impressionable virgins,

in hopes that madness would grip us.

The Language of Wind

First the fan didn't work, then the window wouldn't open. Our torsos hanging out, looked for wind coming hurried, arms outstretched, fingers opened to let it through. Nights when the record high was 108 and we sought anything cool: an opened fridge. Air with sand or even frozen cod was a relief, though sometimes air, any air, carried a cry. We heard it climbing the back of the alley, houses connected by the spine of one long staircase. Smell of urine. Air an illusion gone dingy, dirty. Summer over our bodies like a torch. We treated it like a dream, the sunlight dying. It is how we knew another day had moved on. We only attended to the turn of the fan reaching us in its incessant oscillation; loud, allusive language on our faces. It was love that mattered then, love from friends, and boys gathering, weak from admiration. All this time we could've said, *we have enough.* But we were girls. When no one watched us, we left our bodies to rest on the sofa and took our eyes and wishes to *¡Hola! magazine.*

La edad de la ternura

Every day after classes
we pick up Irene from La Facultad.

That first year when she thought herself a doctor
and tried to help El Pedigüeño with a stick through his hand.

She swore it was her calling, that her parent's voices
were the breath above the store's awning telling her to do it.

She fainted after seeing maggots swim
inside the purple ring of his sore.

Her description, *exactly*.

She held on to her promise for a few
years, to study the body as a curriculum.

The body omits nothing, she'd say.

Nights, we sat in the park after classes,
she quizzing equally

the names of illnesses and of men in her classes.

The nights expanded from
parks to soda bars, to socials
later on,

sweating after dancing to a good
salsa band.

All had music in it!
Sound lifting like bridges around town,
and vessel after vessel of rugged

narrative

passed through our bodies.

Skin taking on the color of rust
as blood rose to the epidermis
and diluted itself in our potion of baby oil
and cinnamon.

Our bodies then:
straight backs
long necks
pert bosoms.

Our hair then: black,
adamant.

Our eyes then:
gazing
herding.

Art Institute

Sonia gets paid to pose,
collarbone slightly
upturned,

rib cage high.

The navel eye
above the dark-lamb hair.

The real eye looks at him
from the side

without the purple birthmark.

An artist's hardest task,
to get flesh color

just right.

He smudges onyx
on top of amber.

Add a hint of red,
he talks to himself

about the limitations on his palette.

Sonia, on How to Fool a Wolf

In the end, I'm still young
and learning

where
to unfold.

I enter his house when the afternoon waivers,
a pigtailed girl

never made holy.

He feels my knee
and I drop

my eyes,
point to a book

and drift—
drift through the room

untouched but watched.

The threshold
is the next
room—

He's by your side again
stuttering
as if something caught in the vacuum

just before the red rug
of his tongue.

And I do not fall in love.

Ideology of Excavation

We paint our nails
and drink aguardiente.
When not in our mouths
the bottle is held with our knees—
crested feet meet on the floor.
From aerial view we could be
pre-Columbian figurines. Pulled out
from dirt, eyes opened inward—
in our arms,
the gated loot of history—
beauties ruined in the de-caving, in the
dis-covery, in the dis-card. In the handling
of a body or face, the brute hand
can be a weapon. Loved ones should've buried
us—tied us to earth—secured us in her pristine lap.

PART II

Matilde and the Walking Dreams,

entering the pop-up club with its gold-trimmed
glass walls. At the oak bar, all the sharks in place,
tough, slangy guys, ready to touch.

You can call them beautiful, *mamacitas*,
or *sirenas*. Watch them strut, skirts pulled tight;
watch how a gorgeous fog expands between their bodies
and the light.

A magic trick: they float slowly, long necked, shoulders
back, across the concrete floor.

Where they came from, they were called the Eves.

Back in the bathroom, they run a baby wipe
over exposed arms, shoulders, and fierce cheeks.

They count their money.
No negotiations: *twenty for a dance, twenty for a dance.*

At the social, every other Friday, they jerk
to the nasal tones of their partners.

Their gaze, a clock on the wall.

Thrift

I learned to love the smell of mothballs,
capped in the air of closets.

My first dress, pink and tight
like liquid skin—

iconic, the cashier said.

Waist set with lilies,
I hemmed it, ironed.

A found button—
almost a match, I told myself.

The day I took it off in front of you.
Arching my spine,

casting *that* shadow
over my face.

And yes, that too—

midday traffic rattled
rolling like a giant marble.

Under His Wing

At the evangelical church
where her parents found a husband
for Matilde at eighteen.

José Augusto,
son of a pastor.

He liked to put his hand
over her mouth when she
contradicted him.

A whole sky of white doves,
her adolescent body,
entering the church as if for her final rest.

Early Settlers

It would be like that—like early settlers working the land.
A good worker; underneath my long skirt

my legs are toned. From squatting.

My waist, a road home; all day I will admire
your arms—how they bundle

and rope.

Who wanted us nomads? God
should have worked harder.

He was in a rush to finish this country,
tired of blowing breath to raise

our skeletal bodies.

Unsolicited (Bird) Love

Let us suppose then
I'm transient, ungraceful,
observant of meaningless truths like:
water in your temples
tastes of iodine and rust.
You promise nothing with that glance
but my joy increases–
Disregarding the *others*
I orbit toward your yellow straw,
your pale thinness
with acrobatic pains.
I speed away from the flock.
Blood pumping–
I must look spectacular–
I stop to breathe over poppies
–eyes iridescent, pitted
blue-green from which earth
seems only a tiny spot.
I show you heart–
pumping.

Summary

There stood love, handsome,
at the promenade, carrying a fish pole.
Not a strange place for love to hang out.
When I made up your face, under the sun,
you must have said a word like *drink*
or *potion.* It was the law of fishing
you talked about.
What is the law of fishing?
But the cease of hope. A fish surrenders,
oscillates between the spiritual
and the tragic. That day was black writing.
Maybe you bought a past life I've forgotten to redeem.
I wanted the world to speak, but it was just me
and my thoughts and iron pressing the chest.
I dug my feet in sand, looped my toes in algae.
Ignored the violent current.

Fall

She doesn't want to brag
about real love
but she married at the county jail
in a blue shirtdress she borrowed
from Irene.
What he promised her, only she knows,
but she is always after it.
One Saturday a month
a bus takes her for a weekend of marital bliss.
A black suitcase with lace
and the green plantains he craves.
She loves his built-up body
and the kiwi tone of his eyes.
His breath is sacred
wind and all other clichés.
This was art: to follow him
as he broke up the law,
until he was stopped by a bullet.
They have nothing left but the ordinary:
a beer, a cigarette shared.
He explains the future to her—

Marital Ode

He says to believe in our future,
we're in the room *he can afford for now.*
There are scratches on his face, drawings
of his whereabouts the night before.
Un cuento, while I slept, while I vanished
behind his fantasies.
He counts once, and again, and then again,
a third time, lifting his head in my
direction. Bills go into the pillowcase.
A naked torso with signs of law bending;
on his cheeks, permanent marks
of teenage acne.
I don't know much of him, but this dance
of fingers—
Another life happens outside, but here
some wild beast is devouring the future.
I stand where two windows dip the same sun.
Love, he calls, but all I hear is life.

Ancient Ceremony

I'm fine with crouching this low
and biting the cloth. I am anointing
you with the water expected of spring days,
when rain is hard and mud garlands
the river. Quick! It's not blood
that holds us together, but the afterbirth.
A skin so transparent, I can see the lobe
of the liver. My hands upon the head,
on the ribs that crisscross over the center
where the heart is eggplant dark. Rest now,
on the gardens of alluvial soil, and let me
rest now. O, the tongue's incessant malice in
naming things. Reverse Moses, then.
Pre-Moses, then. I have gone inside
and ripped me like silk. Thrown the placenta
to prevent another.

Cards

No quietness in the heart / the Sagittarius /
the ancient landmark / foundations / others / built on /

New moon / pulls / like a dog / by the ears / smoke starts / bad hand—

Twilight in a Bathroom Somewhere

Today, this deep obstinate
sadness, from the skies. The big O

to catch air.
In delirium,

as fish,
contorting on a deck.

The weak light runs down the wall
as if dirty water.

What's on my chest
is the shade darker

than nautical dusk,
minutes before

night wins.

Secret

Once I enter the slow wave of another day, what happened there, in that house, the walls with the green flanks, the hall leading to your room, I'll forget. I'll forget the wild elephants I framed late into the dawn hours, remorse thick like an elephant's leg. Remorse I fall over—over the shadow of woman with a child in her arms. A frozen image of us, silent, gesture-less. The body of another woman, the skin you want so badly is not my skin. Just a dream I'll keep dreaming of, deleting myself, little by little.

Notes on the Dead

There are some knots impossible to undo.
Mierda must have been the final word.
I heard the quiet rumor that a bullet
entered his skin and my own mind drilled
it through his forehead.
But the iron intent expanded inside
and he banged his head like a goat on the sidewalk.
It's a good thing he died that fast,
cut from our lives.
Were you bringing us a bag of groceries?
Some yuca bread?
It was the hour of thieves, they tell me.
For me, my dear love, you were never a thief.
But with you dead now, it is something
I need to distinguish.

Black Box

What we felt we couldn't say
and now I light candles for you,

I greet the mornings for you,
the dangling cord with the catch of the day.

They still talk about
how you used to *give them a hand.*

Forearms showing your first scars,
white and rubbery.

You parted—raking
your own ash. That hour of January

when the sky tugged silver fabric
outside the window—the oddest thing.

Each day after, there was a brief
pause to wipe my eyes.

Thinking of the other you
lying on the ruins of hard slab

at the morgue—naked torso
and headdress of iodine and a white sack.

Husband, father.

Death Is Slowly Nesting in Your Body

When you were closer to death
your body already smelled of it.

Your eyes were chipped pebbles.
I saw myself in them,
oddly sketched

in the narrow rim of your partial vision.

How did I look to you, then? I can't remember
except for a picture Irene took of us.

I floated
like a young gray ghost,
malnourished

and fearful.

Late Husband

Sometimes the underworld's leash stretches
further into the living pool.
You rented me your body, let me
fill you with the nickel taste
of a tundra. Where your mouth is missing,
the dross of the earth covers.
You shake the eternal chimes
of leaves as I walk, distracted.
You gather clouds.
With luck, I notice a strange light,
a trick, a face with lidless eyes.
I might shriek, but I understand.
You leave notes in my dreams, and I sniff
the fossil strata of your bones.
A half dozen, between worlds.
How the dead love us.

Go Ahead, Enter

I will stand with you in the cupboards
of the era when you looked the most happy
like the nescient inflatable dogs you made for
our daughter
cobalt and magenta big footed
unbalanced. The sun leading us you
with rotted luggage toward what waited behind
that enamel door
at the edge of sky.
The amateur ways of your new
body, sidelining thirst, and blue,
believing there was music ahead.

PART III

Women at the Margins

Town's hyacinths shouting
from white plastic buckets
at the bus station. We wait.
Early food vendors banging pots;
something always prodded or stabbed.
Cords and pulleys everywhere, but moreover,
men whistling, trading dust.
Dozens of them sweating, running errands.
We wait for other women.
It's too late for regret, lady. Missing flyers.
Later come the flowers!
These two possibilities exist,
the trafficker says; his voice is a whip
of truth.
I watch him while we wait for the rest.
Don't worry, every ride is different. What
he offers me is the terrible charity of pity
for my sin.
I know my sin.
Dark dividing distance.
I know there are tiny hands looking for me
and I don't touch them—your night, my dawn.
It's so dark where I've gone,
wearing night's shade, I want you to know
the first women also walked to trade
their seeds—made eatable,
taxable.
Women move through time and place,
alone in the dark.
Our tongues only kiss when we call
out our children's names, taking pictures
from plastic wallets.
Love has not ended.
Like water that accumulates in a street ditch.

Like sweat, all over,
like creation taking place among abandoned bones
as grass injects itself.

Hunger

In a narrow space between my ribs and my heart
the incessant trapeze artist flipped.

Little Outside Sonnet

You are the terrible hour now, what provokes the disorder
in my veins. You're what shatters in place
of the window. These clouds are giant eyes
upon roofs across a field. I become my own
threatening flow of sadness as your orange
hay light grows, impatient, mouthy. I'm using these lips
as barriers to the tongue's dangerous
landscapes. The wizard verbs in use to describe You.

Convinced an animal races through me as well.
The wood mask that covers you hides a door.
And your hard chest opens to the knock
of a beak, reminding me of the shivering act
of happiness, the momentary scaffolding upon the soul,
rows of infinitives because there is delight in loss.

Progress

The new part of town
was a stranger who never left.

Scoria houses reinforced
to hold rich

colors behind iron masks;
privacy fences that led to gardens

of rock and salt.

People gave each other only
what came boxed, foreign,

and plastic.

And we, *the walking dreams*, spent our time at the Promenade
looking for evidence of luxury where it didn't exist.

Sending wishes across the ocean on
banana leaves.

Wasn't it the fantasy then
to expect someone to answer back?

Mothers and Daughters in Portraits

I grabbed what I could.

No, I grab what I want.

No, I carry my daughter out
to the patio, daylight just wakening,
touching the roof.

Even the sun
knows it needs to be gentle. Keep
her eyes closed and only give warmth,
like a cotton blanket.

I should stay still, hearing
the way silence wants to roll out
from under the sink, from under the tile.

I stand on the square that glues me. All around,
things already look foreign, tasteless,
absurd. I can't wake this child to the promise

of me. I bring her back to bed before she opens
her eyes, recognizes what's hers,
and attempts to claim it back.

A Better Story

Like a prophet, a mother knows how to tell a story.
All answers in one little sentence.

Cats walking at night, split stars.
Without breathlessness, without tears—she talks
distances between daughters and fathers,
she says, *earth, wood.*

Truth being a fragment—
Leaving you was—

Calling a Last Meeting

Yes! Let's take rum to the beach,
lie on sand naked.
Not like before
when we were
stellar relics
shining coconut oil torsos
pancartas.
How do I break from this town?
From my daughter?
Are the purple smudges of my birthmark
God's code?

Bone Harp

We take shelter in dead cows and
lift ourselves with hooks to keep out of sight.
At checkpoints, our dangling bodies
hold legs to chest, as instructed, to avoid detention.
All language snuffed out
by the blue perch of meat. It's a miraculous
thing to be wrapped in it.
After we pass, relief rustles
the epidermis—enough to warm us
for some time.
Who trained our bodies for this?
Poverty is violence.
We know the look of dead
things behind pinned drapes and how to make
history in one day. We bent at the knees
to kiss our children's faces.

Inventory

Five days in the meat locker
and the white yarn of bones I lean
against.
I need my heart to shoot out
like an arrow, to leave the body
by the cobwebs or otherwise
send it back in a cardboard coffin.
I blow air to give love to something—
back home, it's summer.
My toes are numb, and if I am to be
expelled, naked, into this winter and
pounded into a figurine, I want to be the
ballerina.
The thing to believe here is: temporary.
I know it takes time
for God to answer prayers.
Among the cow's ruins, a faint
light. The only form of language I
miss.

Meat Locker Companion

As if he finds his misery
and hunger amazing

he wakes up
with a laugh—a bird

half buried
in the grounds

of his chest.

Guilt Game

Sonia liberates from it,
treats it like any other legend,

La Llorona, or El Duende,
after the blue thread

on her wrists healed,

using cotton and rain
from her eyes.

Perhaps she'd done all she could,
perhaps she can do more.

She spots herself
around in other places

living another life.

Primordial

If again you
fail to calm
hunger

that muttered ache
scrolling

that predator in the mind
like the nacreous eye

of a cat.

Not much left in you
but your own humble spit

and whatever joy is left
in the world—

dying like a wild
animal on a snowless
mountain

or in an empty valley.

Walk, Repeat

A kind of drunk feeling.
Late afternoon, this sun
is now one orange yolk–

I'm so hungry.

Watch us lug our heavy books
of memories.

As Seen from the Sky,

the women on wicker chairs.
Their smoke lands on

tangled lattice mold,
trees,

nylon stockings drying on clotheslines.

Air is kept in the rib cage
of the *mosquitero*.

Dogs always come home to die.

We don't need to know who said that!
Laughter.

The echo of something
that'll stop happening.

Meal Offering

Mañana, mañana, I'll come home
mañana.

Please be kind to my story,
my tales of this desert ordeal.

Bring some bread for memorials
and the incense
of dried dirt.

They'll find rubber soles,
a cross-body bag.

They'll say that after some time
only nails and hair are left.

The first is kept for the secrets,
the other is kept for its smell.

The Divines Talk

Hiding in cloud pockets—their faces
the opaque points in the sky.
Hallucinations, though they mean happening.

We're grouped together, snouts for mouths.
We are noises. Hearts are noises too

thumping steel.

Divines discuss latest data—

To speak plainly,
you don't live your lives right.

Bad–
bad DNA–

We think a curse,
something must have ruined them.

Names of Other Women

Crossing over, names are just ghosts;
there is no list. No name for the child
from Ecuador who asked to go to the bathroom
and hanged herself, like an aborigine flag. Names walk
alone, die alone. Names are silk,
burned by pebbles; sand, ripped by wire.
Names are birds singing indistinguishable
death rhythms only the original womb
can hear.
I talk about names out of questionable archives.
The killing sun, the fast river.
Names come apart in syllables
like *No!* under an accomplice sky.
Names are suffocated or burned.
Names mistake the silhouette
of death for a loved one.
They could only call out to
loneliness at the time of death.
Who said, *Let's not waste*
another tree
on ghost names?

Ways of Translating Horrible Things

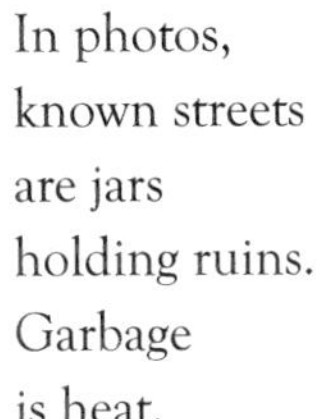

In photos,
known streets
are jars
holding ruins.
Garbage
is heat.

Fear hides under the tongue.

Anger is:
a glance.

Hunger:
an explosive.

Watch how easy
it is to steal
a life.

Some feet never escape
a burned country.

The elation of a journey,
some catch hope

in a fist.

PART IV

In the Late Eighties 400,000 Ecuadorians Migrated to the United States

And not one bird?
        We love our vulture,
        the Andean condor,
        33 pounds massive.
        Black bird with white wings
        bald red head
        male yellow eyes
        who waits in the whiteness
        of mountaintops.
And why did you come here?
        For the lie.

In a Souvenir Sent from Guayaquil

The sun hid inside
the volcano for years: toxins
or woe? Inside the gray ash
saucer top: God's punishment
or indifference?
Someone forgot to pull the skin of night over the town.
Smoke confused for oracles; fear thorny like pine needles.
Life continued, in the pastoral way.
Nothing wrong with the old.
At La Plaza, their hero bent his cast-iron head.
The city, an old pigeon,
confided in its gray plumage.
Ode to the peeling primary colors of houses, flags, and birds.
Ode to the rancid fried fish, yuca, and plantains.
Ode to the Pacific, a force that having crossed the world
came back to see Los Altos.
The harbor wrecked by a wind that comes from absence.
Its language written: *shhhh.*

Strong Gold

Light floods a football field on television.
Strangers to Thanksgiving

our first holiday,
the rite

of passage
feels mundane.

Men watch American football,
footbol, they say.

Not knowing they call out, *¡gol!*
Gold shirts on the field

where a coiled-gold sun
times its own setting.

Call out between the lips
the absent ones—

We are here.
We buy back some dignity,

pearl-shade Corelle plates,
fake heirlooms.

We are in a new state of affection—

New sound:

frozen dew when it gives up
on the fire escape landing.

We lock eyes with gold fake sunflowers
on a vase one of us will want to take when we disperse–

go on.

On the field, a touchdown,
blessed gold T-shirts run across.

We resist our urge to save food.

Our lives have begun–

On Jerome Avenue an abyss of clouds like colored wigs.

You've given us back our lives,
here is a prayer.

The skeleton of a turkey
on a tray.

A Letter from the United States

Running backstreets, Matilde,
Irene, me, until we got to the beach.
How long ago did we learn?
There were no legends
in town.
How many nights did we fantasize
our exiles?
Drawing the escape in sand
with index fingers—
on our knees, the way you would
enter a church, sins heavy
on your shoulders.
We yawned to the hard work of the moon
and ignored the sweet smell of cane
burned into candy.
We lifted Coca-Cola bottles to the
opened granadilla of our mouths.

Acknowledgments

I would like to express deep gratitude to my family, especially my husband, Diego, and my children, Adrianne and Kevin. Thank you for your unwavering support throughout my journey.

To my parents, Beatriz and Luis, who took a chance and migrated to the United States in search of better opportunities. My parents, for whom empathy was essential for a peaceful life. Thank you to my siblings who proudly celebrate the big and small with me.

Gratitude to the New School and the faculty who fostered my work and encouraged me to continue questioning and challenging myself: John Reed, Catherine Barnett, Mark Bibbins, David Lehman, Sharon Mesmer, Laura Cronk, Elaine Equi, and Lori Lynn Turner.

To Eduardo C. Corral, one of the most generous and brilliant faculty members I have had the luck to meet.

To Adrianne Bonilla Stankus, whose brilliant mind can find the unexpected in a line. Thank you for your edits, for your understanding, and for the talent you share with ease.

To the generous teachers I have worked with in many writer's workshops: Garrett Hongo, Jeffrey Levine, Bruce Smith, A. Van Jordan, Patrick Phillips, Ada Limón, Tarfia Faizullah, Bianca Stone, Natalie Shapero, Carl Phillips, Jason Schneiderman, and Eduardo C. Corral.

Genuine gratitude to Bread Loaf Writers' Conference, Tupelo Press, Colgate Writers Conference, the Vermont College of Fine Arts Postgraduate Writers' Conference, the Frost Place (with a special thank you to Martha Rhodes for her support), Tin House, Napa Valley Writer's Conference, Sewanee Writers' Conference, Community of Writers, and Kenyon Review Adult Writers Workshop.

Many thanks to Rigoberto González for your support and understanding of what I was doing and why. Thank you for being a visionary and a benevolent reader of poetry.

Thank you to all the writers I've met throughout the years whom I now consider friends:

Raven Jackson, Maria Richardson, Atoosa Grey, Meghan Dunn, Amy Scheiner, Carlene Kucharczyk, Kirsten Miles, Benjamin Garcia, Eduardo Martinez-Leyva, Laura Grothaus, Rachel Dillon, Elina Katrin, M. Cynthia Cheung, Luciana Arbus-Scandiffio, Angela Siew, Analia Villagra, and María Gómez de León, with whom I shared a University of Notre Dame Letras Latinas Scholarship.

Thank you, Joseph Quintela and Deadly Chaps Press, for giving a home to my MFA thesis, "An Animal Startled by the Mechanisms of Life."

Finally, immense gratitude to the journals that published my poems: *Acentos Review*, *Blackbird*, *Cimarron Review*, *Crosswinds Poetry Journal*, *Green Mountains Review*, *Jet Fuel Review*, *Reed Magazine*, and *RHINO*.

Finally, a thank you note to Eduardo C. Corral, Bianca Stone and Natalie Shapero for reading the book, for seeing me and my poems.

Dedication

For my parents, Beatriz y Luis: You are always with me.
For Diego, Adrianne, and Kevin: I love you.
To my brothers and sisters and to all the family before us who paved the way.

Previously Published

"Market" (now "La Bahía, Guayaquil"), "Fall," *Acentos Review*
"Strong Gold," *Blackbird*

"Ancient Ceremony," *Cimarron Review*

"Go Ahead, Enter," *Cream City Review*
"How to Fool a Wolf," (now "Sonia, on How to Fool a Wolf"), *Crosswinds Poetry Journal*
"La edad de la ternura," *Green Mountains Review*
"Inventory," "Meat Locker Companion," *Jet Fuel Review*
"Language Arts," *Reed Magazine*
"Bone Harp," *RHINO*

About the Author

Silvia Bonilla holds an MFA from the New School. She is the author of the chapbook *An Animal Startled by the Mechanism of Life* (Deadly Chaps, 2014). Her work has been featured in *Blackbird*, *Green Mountains Review*, and *Cream City Review*. She has received support from the Kenyon Review Adult Writers' Workshops, Sewanee Writers' Conference, Napa Valley Writers' Conference, Community of Writers, the Constance Saltonstall Foundation for the Arts, and Juniper Institute.

Helping or Hurting Professions: Mental Health & Substance Abuse Treatment

Howard Coleman Jr, RN, CAP, LCSW

Helping or Hurting Professions: Mental Health & Substance Abuse Treatment